# PROCEEDINGS.

Agreeably to previous notice, a meeting of the colored citizens of Boston was held in the Southac Street Church, on Monday evening, Dec. 17th, 1855, for the purpose of presenting a testimonial to Mr. William C. Nell, for his disinterested and untiring exertions in procuring the opening of the public schools of the city to all the children and youth within its limits, irrespective of complexional differences. The church was crowded by a finely-appearing and evidently intelligent audience, all of whom appeared to take a lively interest in the proceedings.

At half-past seven, the beneficiary was escorted into the church by the Committee of Arrangements, viz.: Mrs. Joanna Turpin Howard, Mrs. Caroline Butler Lewis, Mrs. Eliza B. Bisbitt, Mrs. Georgiana O. Smith, and Mr. Nelson L. Perkins. Mr. Perkins called the meeting to order, which was organized by the choice of the following officers: —

PRESIDENT,

JOHN T. HILTON.

VICE PRESIDENTS,

Jonas W. Clark,
Simpson H. Lewis,
Wm. H. Logan,
George W. Lowther,
Robert Morris, Esq.,
Peter Hawkins,
J. S. Rock, M.D.,
Edwin F. Howard,
Robert Johnson,
William Johnson,
Lewis Hayden,
John Wright,
J. V. DeGrasse, M.D.,
Henry Hatton.

SECRETARIES,

Nestor P. Freeman, George L. Ruffin.

Prayer was offered by Rev. Charles W. Upham, (editor of the *Christian Watchman,*) after which the President briefly addressed the assembly, alluding to the various efforts which had been made for the overthrow of the obnoxious and disgraceful caste school, to the shameful abuse with which these efforts had too often been met, by members of School Committees and others, and to the persistent and patient labors of the friends of the movement, which had at last been brought to a triumphant termination. Among those who had remained faithful to the end, (he said,) might be named William C. Nell, (applause); who, like Moses of old, would not be put off, but, seeing the suffering and hearing the sighing of the children of his brethren, was moved in his inmost soul to resolve that they should not suffer the shame much longer, if any devotion and energy on his part could accomplish their deliverance. With this determination, he went forward, making all the efforts necessary in the case, until success had crowned his labors; and the meeting that evening was for the purpose of presenting to him a testimonial of their appreciation and gratitude. (Loud applause.)

## FLORAL PRESENTATION.

Mrs. Caroline Butler Lewis then came forward and sang a floral invocation, which was repeatedly applauded, and at its conclusion, Master Frederick Lewis, in behalf of the children who have been so highly benefitted by Mr. Nell's labors, addressed him as follows: —

"Champion of Equal School Rights, we hail thee! With unbounded gratitude we bow before thee! Our youthful hearts bless thee for thy incessant labors and untiring zeal in our behalf. We would fain assist in swelling thy praise, which flows from every lip, but this were a tribute far too small. Noble friend! thou hast opened for us the gate that leadeth to rich treasures; and as we pass through, Ambition lendeth us a hand — ay, she quickeneth our pace; and as, obeying her, we look through the vista of future years, we recognise bright Fame in a field of literary glory, her right hand extended with laurels of honor, to crown those who shall be most fortunate in gaining the platform whereon she standeth; while before her is spread the banquet, with viands rich and rare, that our literary hunger may be satiated. To this we aspir

To gain this, we will be punctual to school, diligent in study, and well behaved; and may we be enabled to reach the goal, that, in thy declining years, thy heart may be gladdened by what thine eye beholdeth, and it shall be like a crown of gold encircling thy head, and like a rich mantle thrown around thee, studded with jewels and precious stones.

"Kind benefactor! accept, we entreat thee, this simple token, emblem of the bright, gladsome years of youthful innocence and purity; and as thou hast befriended us, so may we ever prove faithful friends to thee! May the blessings of Heaven attend thee through life's ever-changing scenes and intricate windings, is our prayer.

"*Long live William C. Nell, the noble champion of Equal School Rights!*" (Prolonged cheering.)

On the conclusion of his address, Master Lewis presented Mr. Nell with a beautiful bouquet, and several other children, — Elizabeth Smith, Clarence Howard, Adeline Howard, Charles Guess, Anne Steamburg, Julia Bailey, and Ira Nell Gray, — came forward, each bearing a similar offering. This scene was an exceedingly pleasant one, and the audience expressed their gratification in repeated cheers.

## PRESENTATION OF AN ELEGANT GOLD WATCH.

Mrs. Georgiana O. Smith then, in the following well-spoken address, presented to Mr. Nell a very fine and costly gold watch, as a token of the regard and esteem of his friends, in whose behalf he had so perseveringly labored: —

Mr. Nell, — Dear Sir, — It is with feelings of the deepest emotion that I, in behalf of the colored citizens of Boston, appear before you this evening, to present you this watch, as a token of our esteem and respect for your untiring exertions in securing Equal School Rights for the colored children of the city of Boston.

Sir, it would be difficult for me to describe the heartfelt feelings of respect and gratitude our colored friends of Boston entertain for you; — you, who were never known to swerve from your course, but were always ready when an opportunity occurred to plead and battle for the rights of the people with whom you are identified; — you, who were never weary or disheartened, even when the battle raged fiercest, or the object at which you aimed seemed almost unattainable; even then you persevered, and those who met you, from day to day, saw Hope seated upon your brow, and its light irradiating your countenance. With you, there was "no such word as fail."

And now, knowing these things to be so, I present to you this token of our respect; and may the citizens of Boston always feel a warm regard for this our tried and valued friend, and may the name of WILLIAM C. NELL be handed down to posterity as the champion of Equal School Rights! (Loud cheers.)

The watch bears this inscription: —

"A Tribute to
WILLIAM C. NELL,
FROM THE COLORED CITIZENS OF BOSTON,
For his untiring efforts in behalf of
EQUAL SCHOOL RIGHTS,
Dec. 17, 1855."

## ADDRESS OF MR. NELL.

MR. PRESIDENT, LADIES AND GENTLEMEN:

The struggle for Equal School Rights, which for so long a series of years has taxed our hearts, our heads and our hands, having, through the aid of many friends, at length been triumphantly successful, it was but natural that the gratitude of parents and children should desire to make some record of the emotions awakened by such a signal and public good. With partial kindness, you have been pleased to make me the recipient of these honors, in recognition of the humble services it was my privilege to render the cause we all have loved so well.

Any attempt to express the feelings which swell my heart at this, the proudest moment of my life, it is no affectation to say, would be wholly unavailing. Your own hearts can best interpret mine. To be surrounded by such a constellation of friends from various walks of life, comprising those who have known me from early boyhood, and those of but recent acquaintance — realizing the fact that this is their united testimonial, approving my course in so glorious a reform — to be elaborate on such a theme calls for abilities far transcending any that I possess. I should be doing injustice, however, to my own sense of right, were I to allow the occasion to pass without referring to others, whose words and deeds, in promotion of the movement, should engrave their names indelibly upon the tablets of our memory.

To secure accuracy of names and dates, I have committed them to paper; but, anticipating the mental feast in reserve for us from the distinguished friends who have graced our meeting with their presence, I will be as brief as the circumstances will admit.

In the year 1829, while a pupil in the basement story of the Belknap-street church, Hon. Harrison Gray Otis, then Mayor of the city, accompanied Hon. Samuel T. Armstrong to an examination of the colored school. It chanced that Charles A. Battiste, Nancy Woodson and myself were pronounced entitled to the highest reward of merit. In lieu of Franklin Medals, legitimately our due, Mr. Armstrong gave each an order on Dea. James Loring's Bookstore for the Life of Benjamin Franklin. This is the copy I received! — [a diminutive 18 mo. edition, of some two hundred pages.] The white medal scholars were invited guests to the Faneuil Hall dinner. Having a boy's curiosity to be spectator at the "feast of reason and the flow of soul," I made good my court with one of the waiters, who allowed me to seem to serve others as the fee for serving myself, the physical being then with me subordinate. Mr. Armstrong improved a prudent moment in whispering to me, "*You* ought to be here with the other boys." Of course, the same idea had more than once been mine, but his remark, while witnessing the honors awarded to white scholars, only augmented my sensitiveness all the more, by the intuitive inquiry, which I eagerly desired to express — "If you think so, why have you not taken steps to bring it about?"

The impression made on my mind, by this day's experience, deepened into a solemn vow, that, God helping me, I would do my best to hasten the day when the color of the skin would be no barrier to equal school rights. I need not tell you, that it was several years before any movement could be made promising a favorable result. In the year 1840, Wm. Lloyd Garrison, Wendell Phillips, Francis Jackson, Henry W. Williams, and myself, signed a petition, asking the City Government to grant equal school rights. Of course, but little if any progress was made at that time. In the year 1846, another petition was forwarded from George Putnam and eighty-five others. In 1849, Jonas W. Clark and 227 others renewed the appeal, which was urged through several years, attended with agitations and occasional skirmishes, not always confined to our white citizens, until, in May, 1854, George F. Williams, Esq., submitted an able report to the City Government, recommending equal rights and equal privileges to colored children. His efforts, responded to by a few members of each branch, paved the way for that action in the succeeding Legislature which accomplished the long-sought-for object. As a means to this end, petitions were circulated, and though but to a limited extent, it resulted in 1469 names being forwarded. Of this number, I had the honor of obtaining 311 in Boston, which was augmented by 87, through the exertions of our zealous friend, Lewis Hayden. It will not be invidious to mention two places in the Commonwealth whose earlier and successful struggles in the same reform prompted their ready and cheerful coöperation with us. Wesley Berry headed the one from Nantucket, and the name of Hon. Stephen C. Phillips, with the leading clergymen and officials, graced the other from Salem, with 114 names, — a success achieved by the joint labors of the wife of Charles Lenox Remond, Mrs. George Putnam, formerly of this city, and Miss Charlotte L. Forten, pupil in the Normal School. John B. Bailey and Peter Randolph, in Charlestown, were faithful auxiliaries, and the exertions of white anti-slavery friends in East Bridgewater, Lexington, Bolton and Leominster were no less praiseworthy, some towns, including Lynn and Haverhill, sending 300 names and upwards.

These petitions were promptly responded to by the Legislature. In the House, the bill was ordered to a third reading with an affirmative shout, not more than half a dozen voting audibly in opposition. The Senate as readily coöperated, and the Governor placed his sign manual to the bill, April 28.

To the honor of that Legislature be it recorded, that equal school rights found there a host of strong and valiant supporters; among them, Mr. Kimball, of Salem, and that trio, including the member from Essex, so like a *Prince* in defending Humanity's claim, that eloquent and *Swift* witness against those who would despoil us of our rights, and that other, last mentioned now, but more prominent *then* than all, who was never *Slack* in fulfilling his promises, and whose efforts continued until they were crowned with brilliant success.

The City Government, inspired by the State's laudable example, with commendable haste reversed the action of their predecessors, and acceded to the proposition suggested by one influential member, who remarked that "the colored people had in effect abolished the school themselves, and it would be absurd to refuse to pass the order;" and the vote was sustained by 38 yeas to 6 nays; — thus confirming that saying of a wise man, "There are no limits to the power of an intelligent and determined people." Fortunately, the *Bishop* who superintended at the city educational altar proffered his willing heart and hand to secure to our children what the letter and spirit of the law guaranteed.

D'Aubigné, in his History of the Reformation, says, "Opinions make their progress like the waters that trickle behind our rocks, and loosen them from the mountains in which they rest; suddenly the operation is revealed, and a single day suffices to lay bare the work of years, if not of centuries." How beautifully has this truth been illustrated in the reform we this evening meet to celebrate! — an accumulation of words and deeds dotting its whole history to its culmination.

The two extremes of opinion on the Anti-Slavery question have met in this discussion. Some have expressed opinions, legal and otherwise, favorable to the right, who else had no affinity with the Anti-Slavery cause, We have profited by both.

Hon. Richard Fletcher, Hon. Charles H. Warren, John A. Bolles, Esq., Hon. Stephen C. Phillips, Edmund Quincy, Rev. T. W. Higginson, Rev. Daniel Foster, Rev. E. A. Stockman, Rev. John T. Raymond, Hon. Henry Wilson, Hon. C. T. Russell, acted in unison in promoting this desirable object.

Hon. George S. Hillard and Rev. John T. Sargent, on one occasion, were the only two in the School Board to vote in our favor; and Mr. Hillard, on several occasions since, when his legal duties required otherwise, has volunteered his acquiescence in our appeal.

Benjamin F. Roberts, in 1849, instituted a suit against the city for excluding his child from the public schools, which was nobly defended by Hon. Charles Sumner, whose argument, though not then influencing the Supreme Bench, had a most potent bearing on the Legislature which granted our rights. Associated with him in this case was Robert Morris, Esq., whose very presence as a colored member of the Massachusetts Bar, was a living protest against all exclusive colored institutions.

The brothers Francis and Edmund Jackson, and those other

brothers, Henry I. and William I. Bowditch, each pair like Dickens's brothers Cheeryble, were especially active, rivalling each other in these kind offices.

John A. Andrew, with a keen eye to the emergency, amended the legislative bill, making assurance doubly sure.

Wendell Phillips, Esq., from the moment of signing the first petition with Wm. Lloyd Garrison, like him has always been ready, in and out of season, with his rich gifts of voice and pen, before legislative and other committees, to advocate our claims. Rev. Theodore Parker, who stood side by side with Wendell Phillips in those memorable struggles to rescue Thomas Sims and Anthony Burns from the hell of American slavery, placed his name side by side with that of Mr. Phillips on the Boston petition for equal school rights; and, but for an imperative engagement on the part of Mr. Parker, they would have been side by side here this evening, to receive our unfeigned thanks for their abundant labors in this cause.

William J. Watkins also buckled on his armor, and did most efficient service; and you, Sir, our worthy Chairman, your white plume, like that of Henry IV. at the battle of Navarre, was always seen at that point where the blows fell thick and fast in our defence. I am aware how notorious it is that the good man shrinks from the open proclamation to his face of his really good qualities. But while the friends present will not doubt my veracity in these statements, they, and those who have helped rear for us and our children the Temple of Equality, will indulge me on this special occasion, in view of the past, present, and future history of school rights. Let us not forget to duly honor those who, by their exertions, have secured to us these blessings.

While I would not in the smallest degree detract from the credit justly due the *men* for their conspicuous exertions in this reform, truth enjoins upon me the pleasing duty of acknowledging that to the *women*, and the *children* also, is the cause especially indebted for success.

In the dark hours of our struggle, when betrayed by traitors within and beset by foes without, while some men would become lukewarm and indifferent, despairing of victory, then did the women keep the flame alive, and as their hopes would weave bright visions for the future, their husbands and brothers would rally for a new attack upon the fortress of Colorphobia. Yes, Sir, it was the MOTHERS

(God bless them!) of these little bright-eyed boys and girls, who, through every step of our progress, were executive and vigilant, even to that memorable Monday morning, (Sept. 3, 1855,) the trial hour, when the colored children of Boston went up to occupy the long-promised land. It was these mothers who accompanied me to the various school-houses, to residences of teachers and committee-men, to see the laws of the Old Bay State applied in good faith.

An omnipresent consciousness of my own experience when a school-boy, and how my heart would have leaped in the enjoyment then of equal school rights, has proved a strong incentive to my interest for your boys and girls; for, having none of my own, I took the liberty of adopting them all as my children, — and the smiles of approbation with which so many of them have greeted me in their homes and the highways and byways of life, have imparted to me a wealth of inspiration and encouragement not obtainable from any other source. He that makes glad the heart of a child, receives in return whole volumes of benedictions, and is richer far than if upon his brow were entwined a monarch s diadem.

These mothers have also labored at home to instil into the minds of their children the necessity of striving to obtain, as also to appreciate, those rights, — emulating that New England mother who was said to mingle instruction in her children's bread and milk, and put good morals into their apple pies! With commendable zeal, the boys and girls have endeavored to profit by these counsels.

On the morning preceding their advent to the public schools, I saw from my window a boy passing the exclusive Smith School, (where he had been a pupil,) and, raising his hands, he exultingly exclaimed to his companions, "*Good bye for ever, colored school! To-morrow we are like other Boston boys.*"

In my daily walks, I behold the companionship, in studies and healthful glee, of boys and girls of all colors and races in these temples of learning, so justly a theme of pride to every citizen; sights and sounds indeed to me chief among ten thousand, and altogether lovely. And since the 3d of September to the present time, the sun, moon and stars are regular in their courses! No orb has proved so eccentric as to shoot madly from its sphere in consequence, and the State House on Beacon Hill, and old Faneuil Hall, remain as firm on their bases as ever.

This union of mothers and children with husbands and fathers has contributed vastly to the great result. They have been the *allied* forces which conquered our Sevastopol.

To the colored boys and girls of Boston it may now in truth be said, The lines have fallen to you in pleasant places. Behold, you have a goodly heritage! May it stimulate you to heed the voice of Wisdom, as she sweetly offers the choicest treasures of her gathered stores:

"With eager hand the glowing page to turn,
To scan the earth and cleave the distant sky,
And find the force that holds the planets in their spheres."

Do not waste your spring of youth in idle dalliance, but plant rich seeds to blossom in your manhood, and bear fruit when you are old. The public schools of Boston are the gateways to the pursuits of honor and usefulness, and if rightly improved by you, the imagination almost wearies as future prospects dawn upon its vision; for

"Hills peep o'er hills, and Alps on Alps arise."

In response to your floral tribute, so pleasing and acceptable, allow me to say, that I needed it not as an evidence of your satisfaction with the rights obtained, or my participancy therein, for the pleasure of the service has abundantly rewarded me. Endeavor to retain the impressions made upon your memories by this meeting, for, after all, you children are the parties benefitted. Your parents have labored to achieve this good for you, and to them you must ever render due honor. The three children of an Eastern lady were invited to furnish her with an expression of their love before she went on a long journey. One brought a marble tablet, with the inscription of her name; another presented her with a garland of flowers; the third entered her presence, and thus accosted her:—"Mother, I have neither marble tablet nor fragrant nosegay, but I have a *heart*. *Here* your name is engraved; *here* your name is precious; and this *heart*, full of affection, will follow you wherever you travel, and remain with you wherever you repose." I know of no more appropriate advice to boys and girls than to commend their imitation of that child's example; and when a few short years shall have rolled away, and all proscription shall have done its work in the land, may

"You love at times to pause, and strew the way
With the wild flowers that luxuriant pend
From Spring's gay branches, that whene'er you send
Your Memory to retrace your pilgrimage,
She by those flowers her winding course may bend,
Back through each twilight and each weary stage,
And with those early flowers wreathe the white brow of age."

I could cull from my chapter of experience and observation many an unkind and insulting remark uttered against the rights of colored children in Boston, by school-committee men, editors, and others occupying responsible positions; but, as they can be reserved for future use, to "point a moral," if *not* to "adorn a tale," let us, in this hour of victory, be magnanimous enough to cover with the charity of our silence, the names of *all* who have opposed us.

MADAM: In accepting this elegant token from your hands, I am not vain enough to monopolize the honor and gratitude so eminently due to those I have mentioned, and others who have promoted this great work. Let it be regarded as a joint offering to them all, to be held in trust by me only so long as I am faithful to the elevation of those with whom I am identified by complexion and condition — the cause of humanity.

May we all *Watch* each other, that our *hands* may be diligent — our *hours* consecrated, each *minute*, indeed, every *second* in that movement upon our *dial-plate*, indicating a *chain* of Human Brotherhood. The associations of this evening will be my *main-spring*, henceforward — its recollections more fragrant than *choice flowers* — ever-enduring as *time!* Friends, go on!

"Oft as the memories of this hour return,
May friendship's flame within your bosoms burn,
And hand in hand, improvement's course pursue,
Till scenes of earth have faded from your view;
Then your glad spirits, freed from bonds of clay,
Shall soar triumphant to the home of day —
Where softer dews than Hermon's give perfume
To flowers sweeter than in Sharon bloom;
Entrancing music breathe in airs divine,
And toil no more the spirit's flight confiine;
But ever onwards through its bright abode,
Bask in the presence of its Maker, God."

Mr. Nell's address was frequently interrupted by applause, especially at the mention of those anti-slavery friends who had given their aid to the cause.

## SPEECH OF CHARLES W. SLACK.

CHARLES W. SLACK, Esq., of Boston, was then introduced to the audience, and welcomed with hearty and enthusiastic cheers. He said he should not detain them long from the treat which he knew they were anticipating in the addresses of those who were to follow him. He had come there, as they had, simply to express his kindly feeling towards the beneficiary of the evening, — their friend, Wm. C. Nell, — who, as they all knew from their own observation and experience, had been long engaged in the cause of equal school rights for colored youth. He (Mr. S.) felt that this was an evening of jubilee; that they ought all to be thankful that one more prejudice was at last driven from the sanction of the city of Boston. (Cheers.) How singular it was, as had been well remarked on another occasion by the worthy pioneer in the Anti-Slavery cause, [Wm. Lloyd Garrison,] that when, after long years of toil and sacrifice, a victory has been achieved, it has seemed as though no one cared at all for what had been done! It had been especially so with regard to the colored race. The idea had been rigidly entertained by a large portion of the community, that there was something repulsive in having the little children of color sit side by side with those of white parents in the public schools; but when the reform was accomplished, — when, on the first Monday of September last, these bright little ones about us went up, with equal privileges and equal freedom, to the common schools, although, for a moment, there was a slight buzz of astonishment at the unusual spectacle, the next day it had all passed away, and they were met as gladly by teachers and pupils as any other children. He had just been told by one of the School Committee present on the occasion, [Henry Upham, Esq.,] that the teachers in those schools where the colored children are the more numerous, report that they come as neatly dressed, and are as gifted in application and understanding, as the children of parents who have had all the advantages which wealth, position and culture could give! (Applause.)

Well, this prejudice against colored children in the public schools has been driven out of sight — thank God for that! (Cheers.) It was another of the triumphs which had marked the struggle for the elevation of the colored race in this Commonwealth. First came the abrogation of the laws against intermarriage — not that many desired that privilege, but they could not consent that a mark of inequality should be placed upon either race, white or black; then the "Jim Crow" car was abolished, and the privilege of travel in every public conveyance fully maintained; then the places of amusement were thrown open to the colored race equally with the white; then followed, in Boston, the abolition of the "negro pew" in the City Directory, and the record of all the citizens alike, without distinction of color or race; and now, to crown the whole, we have established the right of the humblest child in the community to all the benefits of our common-school education, equally with the offspring of the proudest citizen in the Commonwealth.

He (Mr. S.) regarded this reform only as the stepping-stone to other successes. He hoped the time was not far distant when we should see our colleges and higher seminaries of learning graced by the sable countenances of those who had heretofore been proscribed; and with this recognition of the manhood of the colored race, we should have further advancement in the same direction. By thus recognising their rights in every sphere of life, something would be done towards breaking down that great system of human servitude which is the shame of our land. (Cheers.)

He had remarked on a former occasion, that it was a very singular and somewhat unexpected thing to find so many anti-slavery men in the last Legislature. He did not know how it happened, — whether by the providence of God or the accident of politics, — but *they got there*, and (having an instinctive consciousness that they might never get there again) some of them resolved, if there was any way in which they could make their mark on that Legislature, they would do it! (Loud and prolonged cheering.) Nationally, they thought they had accomplished their mission when they elected HENRY WILSON (cheers) to the United States Senate. That, however, was done so easily, they thought they might try the temper of the House a little further; and so an Address was presented for the official decapitation of Judge Loring, for his unseemly participation in the rendition of Anthony Burns. All knew what was the result of that measure; but he believed that if, under the Constitution, the Legislature had had the power, they would have carried that Address through by a two-thirds vote, over the veto of the Governor, as they did, a little later, the Personal Liberty Bill. These measures disposed of, the anti-slavery members cast about for something that should indicate their direct connection with the colored race, and they found nothing that seemed better suited for their advocacy, than the measure for securing equal school rights to all the children in the Commonwealth. And when Mr. Nell came up with his huge budget of papers, it was a very simple thing to put the manifold testimony he brought into the shape of a "Report," and present it to the House. It was as if an enterprising builder should bring his timber and bricks and mortar into the street, and then, calling in his master-workman, should say to him — "Here, I have got all the material and implements ready, and will furnish the capital needed; now go on and erect the building." It would be an easy matter to do so. And so Mr. Nell furnished all the materials and the capital in this case, and there had risen up, under the direction of the master-workman of the Committee, this fair fabric of equality in the education of the colored youth of this Commonwealth.

In conclusion, Mr. Slack said — "Friends! I know you are all pleased. We have done a good thing; and let us still continue our efforts in the future, ever bearing in mind that we have other duties to discharge in the same direction; and among them, as citizens of a boasted *free* Republic, is, to proclaim, by *act* as well as voice, in the language of our Declaration of Independence, that 'ALL MEN ARE CREATED EQUAL.'" (Loud cheers.)

## SPEECH OF WENDELL PHILLIPS, ESQ.

Mr. PHILLIPS (who was received with loud cheers) said he rejoiced very heartily in the occasion that called them together. It was one of those rare days in the history of a hard struggle, when there was something palpable to rejoice at. Men were always asking — What has the Anti-Slavery agitation done? He was glad they had this answer to make now — It has opened the schools: for he supposed every one would be willing to allow, that without this agitation of the public mind, on the general question, the doors of the schools would never have been opened. When he first took hold of this enterprise, he believed the colored people would never obtain equality in the Senate-house until they got it on the school-bench; and when they got it on the school-bench, if they improved their privileges, they might force what they chose from the community. But two things rule in this country — brains, and money; and brains make money, too, therefore, they are the better. The common schools give one the free and best use of his brains, now, having that, let the colored man get the money; and then he need not ask the white race to let him be equal, for when the white man found the man of color passing him in the race, he would whisper — "By-the-by, that fellow is fully my equal." (Applause.)

He was glad this reform had been carried for another reason.

He was tired of having Mr. Nell come to him with his petitions. (Laughter.) Mr. Nell never could be found without them. He (Mr. P.) was glad he had got rid of him, and was quite willing to take free schools instead.

This victory over which they had met to rejoice was indeed a great gain; it was a basis for something else, and something better still. This struggle reminded him to urge upon them union among themselves wherever their rights were concerned. He remembered that, on one occasion, when, with two or three others, he went up before a Senate Committee, they drafted a bill which the friends of equal rights knew would not secure their object, and they told the Committee so. But the Chairman of the Committee, a Boston lawyer, said — "I know it; but you know, as well as I do, that Boston has determined to have colored schools, law or no law, and you will take that law or none." That man was reëlected to the Legislature by the colored men of Boston! Had they thrown a united vote against him, the man who had thus dared to insult them through their representatives would never have entered that State House again; and his absence would have been the best argument that could have been offered for giving to colored citizens their rights.

The opposition to this movement always came from the city of Boston. He remembered that at one time he appeared before a Legislative Committee, when the Chairman came from the Connecticut Valley, and as he (Mr. P.) began to show that colored schools were illegal, the Chairman interrupted him by saying — "You need not undertake to prove that I have got a nose on my face. Show me that such schools exist, and I will report such a bill as you desire." Nevertheless, his report was worth nothing, for the Boston members opposed it.

The best thing learned by these struggles is, how to prepare for another. They were in for the war. He should never think Massachusetts a State fit to live in, until he saw one man, at least, as black as the ace of spades, a graduate of Harvard College. (Cheers.)

He had no notion of such an empire as ours affected to be, confined to one race — it is too narrow. He did not go for annexing territory only, but for annexing hearts — all sorts of races, all sorts of customs. Let a man burn the dead body of his wife, if she desires it! When they had high schools and colleges to which all classes and colors were admitted on equal terms, then he should think Massachusetts was indeed the noblest representative of the principles that planted her.

They were greatly indebted to the young man whom they had met to honor. These reforms are apt to stop, when everybody's business is nobody's business. They were none of them willing to give the cheerless, disheartening toil, the unremitting industry, the hope against hope, which he has given. If he had not been the nucleus, there would have been no cause; if he had not gone up to the Legislature, when it seemed mere impertinence to go there, nobody would have gone. He (Mr. P.) loved to have these hours, when they could turn away from the battle, to do honor to the self-devotion, to the life-long energy and true-heartedness of such a man. They knew that while many who started with him had been turned aside by professional emolument, or private gain, he had been true to his race, true to his idea. Emerson had said — "A Tory is a Democrat gone to seed." (Laughter.) Cold-hearted age is the natural successor of enthusiastic youth. We see it so often, we expect it. When he saw an old man with the lava of his young enthusiasm just as hot, his confidence in the right just as loyal, his determination to stereotype honest pulses into statutes, just as fixed, as at nineteen, he was the man whom he would point the young to imitate, and the old to try to go back and be like. (Loud cheers.) We say sometimes, distrustfully, "This man has not attended to his own interest; he did not know his own business; he would have been a richer man if he had been more stingy." So he would! It was *our* interests he was attending to; it was the foundation of better times he was laying. It was not the want of sense, it was a higher sense. Their friend Nell had invested his capital in the children of his fellow-citizens, in the ideas which will prevail hereafter; and when he goes down to the grave, those whom he has benefitted will remember and honor him, as one who trusted in the honesty of Massachusetts, and who waited to prove she could be just.

And here I wish to mention with fitting praise the volume, "Colored Patriots of the Revolution," which Mr. Nell has just published. The subject is one which has engaged his attention for many years. The facts lay scattered and difficult of access. With patient diligence, with a watchfulness which has never allowed any opportunity to slip which promised him an addition to his materials, he has, like Scott's Old Mortality, done good service in perpetuating the memories, and refreshing our recollections of the good deeds of those whose fame you ought not to let die. I commend his work most heartily to your patronage. Let it be so generous that others of your young men may be encouraged to like efforts, and specially to gather and preserve the materials for the History of the Colored Race in the United States, — a story which, for thrilling interest and philosophical value will rarely, if ever, be equalled. It is for you now to gather the materials for that History. I hope your young men will make early use of their education and leisure for that and similar purposes, even if, like Mr. Nell, they do so persevering alone, unaided, poor, and at their own cost. But it is in your power to change this picture, and help them and him in these labors by generous and sympathising aid.

There was another reason, Mr. Phillips said, why he rejoiced in this triumph. Some seven years ago, he told the Legislature, when he asked them to go for Disunion, that they must not be tired nor frightened, for the Abolitionists would come year after year and ask it, and we should gain it in the end. (Loud cheers.) And his reason was, that they had gained all they had ever asked for, except Disunion and equal schools. He should only have to make one exception now. It is a fate! The moment a colored man and an Abolitionist sign a petition, it is fated — it will be granted in the end. They might just as well say — these proud legislators, up above the reach of the tide — with the coon, "Is this Capt. John Scott? — for if it is, I will come down," — because they will have to come down in the end! (Laughter and applause.) The next time he met them, he should report progress, and say he attended this meeting, which was another proof he was right. (Cheers.)

## SPEECH OF WM. LLOYD GARRISON.

Mr. Garrison was enthusiastically applauded as he took the platform. He said that, having just returned from a long journey, and from unremitted public labors during the past week, he found himself completely jaded out, in body and mind; but he had promised to be there that evening, and he had gladly come to redeem his pledge.

In the first place, he desired to report progress, as it respected the glorious cause of Anti-Slavery. He had just attended the annual meeting of the Pennsylvania A. S. Society, in the city of Philadelphia. The meetings were characterised by great unity of spirit, and entire order on the part of all who attended, though the most radical doctrines that could possibly be uttered were proclaimed and enforced. It was scarcely nine years since "Pennsylvania Hall," dedicated to Liberty, Justice and Humanity, was consumed to ashes by the torch of pro-slavery incendiaries, merely because the Abolitionists were at that time advocating only the abstract doctrine of immediate emancipation. Yet now, with their doors thrown wide open, and with Southern slaveholders and medical students present, they had been able to rebuke the pro-slavery religion of the land, to repudiate the Constitution, and to demand the immediate dissolution of the Union; and not in any case was the slightest manifestation of hostility or dissent apparent. (Applause.) This was indicative of a great change in public sentiment in that quarter.

Judge Kane found, in their meetings, and in the city, "none so poor to do him reverence," and the strongest denunciations of his conduct, in the case of Passmore Williamson, elicited the warmest approval. He had heard an anecdote which illustrated how the young ideas were learning to shoot, in regard to that infamous Judge. A little boy was catechised after this sort: — "Who was the first man?" "Adam," was the reply. "Who was the first woman?" "Eve." "And who was the first murderer?" "Judge Kane!" (Laughter and applause.)

After what had been said by way of deserved eulogy upon his friend Mr. Nell, and upon the subject of equal school rights, nothing further was needed at his hands, except most heartily to endorse it all. He had been familiar with the history of Mr. Nell from an early period in the Anti-Slavery movement; and he had ever found him true to principle and duty. Their friend was a very modest and diffident man; and this would restrain him (Mr. G.) from saying in his presence, by way of panegyric, all that he might desire to express in his absence. They were now celebrating a victory of far-reaching importance, achieved in a good degree through Mr. N.'s indefatigable efforts, and tendering to him their warmest thanks, and also a valuable token of their regard. Such an hour was always a trying one to an unselfish spirit, because it is much easier to stand up under the rebuffs of open enemies, than it is to receive the plaudits of generous friends.

Mr. Garrison said that he rejoiced that the prejudice against color was dying out, as a result of the Anti-Slavery struggle. The victory they had achieved went to prove what the Abolitionists had so often affirmed, that the color of the skin has nothing at all to do with this prejudice, except, for the time being, to identify the victim to be hated and proscribed. The moment it was bravely coped with, and the struggle became successful, nobody dreamed of talking about the impossibility of whites and blacks mingling fraternally together. When George Thompson, of England, was in this country, he used to tell an anecdote, illustrating this matter of prejudice. While travelling one day in New Hampshire, he met, in a stage-coach, Hon. Salma Hale, who was one of the Commissioners appointed to determine the boundaries between New Hampshire and Maine. He said that, while engaged in this duty, Mr. Hale and his companion had penetrated far into the wilderness, entirely away from all habitations. At length, however, they came to a solitary hut, in which they found a lone woman, her husband being absent in quest of game. As they were both very hungry, they asked the woman if she could give them something to eat. She replied that she could give them some bear's meat. Mr. Hale's companion had a "prejudice" against bear's meat, so he asked her if she could not give them something else. "Well," said she, "I have got some mince pies." "That will do," said the gentleman; "I am excessively fond of mince pies." So the woman brought on the pies, and the stranger was soon eating voraciously, eulogizing the pies in the most emphatic strain. At length, the woman, thinking he must be speaking in irony, said, apologetically, "What can you expect of a poor woman out here in the woods, with nothing to make pies of but bear's meat?" "What!" exclaimed the gentleman, "do you mean to say that these pies were made of bear's meat!" "Certainly," said the woman. "Well, then," said he, "I don't care if I take that other remaining piece." (Laughter and applause.) So, the whites will, by and by, be calling for more colored children, instead of excluding them from our common schools, so ashamed will they be of their ridiculous prejudices. This prejudice is not in nature,— it does not belong to the human race, — and therefore it ought to be put away, at once and for ever.

The victories of the colored people and their friends, over the enemies of impartial freedom, had been numerous and signal; but they had been achieved by rare fidelity and unfaltering perseverance, and by seemingly the feeblest instrumentalities. No great reform was ever projected or early espoused by any powerful organization at the outset. It begins in the heart of a solitary individual; humble men and humble women, unknown to the community, without means, without power, without station, but perceiving the thing that ought to be done, loving the right above all things, and having faith in the triumph of what is just and true, engage in the work, and by and by, the little leaven leavens the whole lump; and this is the way the world is to be redeemed. We have, said Mr. Garrison, every thing to encourage us in a firm adherence to principle. We have never made an issue, as it regards the cause in which we are engaged, in which we have not at last succeeded. It is impossible to do a right act, and be defeated. The enemy may seem to triumph, but it is only a seeming; the truth, in the end, will get the victory.

Among our triumphs, the abolition of all complexional distinctions in the schools of Boston — an event we are here to commemorate — is particularly encouraging. The struggle has been a long and severe one with the pride, the wealth, the aristocratic refinement of the city; but these have been vanquished, and all parties are now reconciled to the change as beneficial, right and proper. And this is but the beginning of the end — the prophecy of the ultimate extinction of complexional caste throughout the land, and of the reign of peace and liberty universally. To our vigilant and untiring friend, Mr. Nell, a large share of the credit belongs for this great victory; and this public recognition of his efforts is as creditable to our colored fellow-citizens as it is worthily his due.

In conclusion, Mr. Garrison expressed his gratification at seeing the Chairman (Mr. Hilton) present, who, he said, had never been found wanting in intelligent discrimination as to the best course to be pursued in the Anti-Slavery movement, and who had ever been ready to do his utmost in behalf of the cause, without compromise or fear. God grant, (said Mr. G.,) that you, my old and cherished friend and supporter, may live to see, with your own eyes, the day of jubilee! And may we all be permitted to join in that glorious celebration! Be assured, we will have freedom yet; we will have free soil and free institutions yet. There is no going back — not a hair's breadth; but "Onward!" is our motto. We will do to the slaveholders, in regard to our Republic, what Jesus did to the money-changers in the temple: we will take the scourge of truth, and drive them out, and there shall not be a tyrant left on our soil. (Loud cheers.)

## SPEECH OF CHARLES LENOX REMOND.

Mr. Remond (who, on coming forward, was warmly applauded) said that he had come up from Salem for the purpose of attending that meeting, and he hoped this fact would be accepted as a slight indication of the interest he felt in the Anti-Slavery cause, and as a testimony that he shared in the feelings which had called that large assembly together. To effect this reform in the matter of school rights had required a great deal of self-sacrifice and the performance of much drudgery, and he was glad that his friend Nell had been called here to receive these testimonials at the hands of his colored friends for the work he had performed.

He thanked God for this occasion, and took courage. He regarded it as one indication that the colored people were beginning to understand the necessity of adhesiveness and consistency—qualities in which, he thought, they had hitherto been lamentably deficient. The day that should witness union among the colored people would witness strength among them, and a general victory, not only over prejudice, but over slavery. (Loud cheers.)

But while they had come up there to congratulate each other on the victory they had achieved, they should be careful to make it understood that they were not yet satisfied with the state of things in Massachusetts. While he admitted, with Mr. Phillips, that this victory afforded a basis for further efforts, he should continue to feel uneasy in his native State while there was a single act of proscription on the part of the white people against the colored people. They must bear in mind that they were yet excluded from the jury box; and he hoped that the colored people of Boston and of the State would commence a new agitation, and not allow it to cease until colored men are seated in the jury box, — at least, on every occasion when a colored man is to be tried. (Prolonged cheering.) In England, when a foreigner was put on trial in a court of justice, one half of the jury were composed of foreigners. They ought to insist here, that when a colored man was tried, one half of the jury should also be colored.

There were certain things which, Mr. Remond said, he wanted the colored people to do, whether the whites desired it or not. They had been accustomed te refer to the judgment of their white friends, but there were certain questions upon which the judgment of the colored man was the best, because the peculiarity of his position better fitted him to understand them.

Mr. R. said he hoped that when they left that house, they would go away with a firm resolution, that wherever there was a difficult duty to be performed in the Anti-Slavery cause, they would assist in its performance, as well as rejoice in the hour of triumph. And when they should do this, they would strengthen the hands and hearts of their white friends. He had no sympathy with the plea that was now made by some, that the colored people should take their cause into their own hands. He held that the Anti-Slavery cause was as much the cause of the white man as of the colored man, for the moment a white man became thoroughly identified with the cause, he was subjected to the same odium and the same insults as the colored man. He trusted he should live to see the day when the last shackle should fall from the last slave in this country; but he should not see it until greater sacrifices were made by the colored people, — until they should learn to value that which was valuable. A great work was yet before them, and they should resolve to do their duty; and if the white man attempted to brow-beat them, let them stand up before him; and if he was determined to drive rough-shod over them and their rights, let them, like the Athenian youth, throw themselves under the wheels of his chariot, resolved rather to die in the spirit of freemen, than live slaves. (Loud applause.)

Some twenty years' experience in the Anti-Slavery cause had taught him one thing — to try and be satisfied with his native country, believing that truth, right and liberty will yet prevail. It would be a burning shame, after what the colored people have suffered in this country, if they should turn their backs upon it. They ought rather to remain here, to demand their rights, and testify to all the world that, with the recognition of those rights, they dare do all that other men dare do. There was a time when he took a pride in the patriotism of colored men in the early history of this country; but he thought now that they made a mistake in fighting for the country at that time, and he thought that, if there should be a war now, it would be a mistake for the colored people to take part in it, except on condition that all their rights were granted to them.

Mr. R. said he longed to see the day when it would no longer be possible for any man or woman to point to pro-slavery colored churches, and to the spirit of colored women who send their children to pro-slavery schools, as evidences of inconsistency on their part. When these things could no longer be said of the people of color, a great work would be done for the overthrow of American slavery. No pro-slavery Committee or anti-slavery Committee would then extend an invitation to slaveholders to address a respectable audience in the city of Boston. He wanted it understood that the colored people regarded such things as insults to them, whatever the motive might be. He wanted Anti-Slavery to become so radical throughout the State, that if the slaveholder came here, he should not be invited to address public audiences, or feasted and toasted in private, but should be obliged to sneak through the community, lest it should be known that he was a slaveholder. (Prolonged cheering.) When this should be the case, he should feel that they were approaching that day which was to witness the deliverance of the slave from his chains.

In making these remarks, Mr. Remond said he did so in no invidious spirit towards any Committee. He wanted the slaveholder made disreputable in the community where colored people lived; and it was in their power so to act, that any Committee would consider it an insult to their intelligence and patriotism to invite the slaveholder into their midst.

In conclusion, Mr. Remond said — "Mr. President, the colored people in Boston must resolve to take more anti-slavery newspapers; they must resolve to contribute more dollars; they must resolve to honor those who devote themselves to their cause; they must resolve to make common cause with those who are laboring in their behalf, and then the work will be comparatively light, and we shall accomplish it the sooner. I look over England, France, Germany, Hungary, Poland, and I see those who consider themselves downtrodden, in each and all of those countries, taking advantage of the present agitation on the great question of liberty or slavery, and resolving to do more than before to secure their emancipation. Let the colored people of this country be but united under a common principle of action, and resolved zealously to labor in its behalf, and all will yet be well. (Loud applause.)

Mr. Garrison said he was gratified and thankful that their friend Remond, while recognising a victory that had been won, had not forgotten the work that yet remained to be done. They ought now to join heart and hand in an appeal to the Legislature to demand that all laws in the Southern States which forbid colored seamen from the North going to the South shall be repealed, and in a way that shall show they are in earnest. The South should be made to understand, that if this is not possible for Massachusetts within the Union, then she will make it possible *without the Union.* (Great applause.)

The following note from Rev. THEODORE PARKER was then read by one of the Secretaries: —

BOSTON, Dec. 17, 1855.

WM. C. NELL, ESQ.:

DEAR SIR,—I regret exceedingly that an engagement to lecture at Framingham will deprive me of the pleasure I had anticipated, in attending the meeting of your countrymen and friends, this evening. I hoped to be with them and you on so joyous an occasion; but as it is impossible, allow me to say, that I think none of your many friends has a higher opinion of your faithful, continuous and modest services to your townsmen and your race, than

Yours, truly, THEODORE PARKER.

The benediction was then pronounced by Rev. L. A. GRIMES, and the exercises terminated.

---

☞ We learn that the morning after the meeting, Mr. NELL received from Mrs. H. B. STOWE an elegant copy of the illustrated edition of "Uncle Tom's Cabin," with the following note: —

"Mrs. Stowe desires to present to Mr. Nell this small addition to the tribute of last evening, regretting that an unfortunate accident prevented its being presented on that occasion.

"May those benefits of education which Mr. Nell has helped to secure for his people bring forth an abundant harvest!

"BOSTON, Dec. 18, 1855."

www.ingramcontent.com/pod-product-compliance
Lightning Source LLC
LaVergne TN
LVHW011145110826
845150LV00008B/2527

* 9 7 8 1 4 1 8 1 9 1 9 5 5 *